VAGRANT

MAKE YOUR LIFE EASIER WITH VAGRANT. MASTER VAGRANT FAST AND EASY.

By Matthew Gimson

Table of contents

Disclaimer

While all attempts have been made to verify the information provided in this book, the author does assume any responsibility for errors, omissions, or contrary interpretations of the subject matter contained within. **The information provided in this book is for educational and entertainment purposes only. The reader is responsible for his or her own actions and the author does not accept any responsibilities for any liabilities or damages, real or perceived, resulting from the use of this information.**

The trademarks that are used are without any consent, and the publication of the trademark is without permission or backing by the trademark owner. All trademarks and brands within this book are for clarifying purposes only and are the owned by the owners themselves, not affiliated with this document.

Introduction

Vagrant can be used for creation and configuration of virtual machines for computers. With the current versions of the software, improvements have been made. As per now, the software is not tied to VirtualBox, meaning that it can work with virtualization software such as KVM or VMware. Although the software was developed in Ruby, it supports projects that were developed in other programming languages. With the software, you can access both private and public networks. You will use the IP addresses reserved for the particular space. The process of creating virtual machines in Vagrant is easy since you are able to use base images. These will guide you during the process, and they are called boxes.

Chapter 1- Definition

Vagrant is computer software used for creation and integration of virtual environments. It is considered a higher-level wrap around software for virtualization such as KVM, VirtualBox, Vmware, and Linux containers, and around software for configuration management like Chef, Ansible, Puppet, and Salt.

After the version 1.1 of this software was released, this software was freed from VirtualBox, and it is able to work with other virtualization software, like the KVM and the VMware. It can also support server environments.
Note that Vagrant was written in Ruby, as stated above. Therefore, it cannot support products written in other programming languages such as Python, PHP, Java,or C#.

With version 1.6 of Vagrant, Docker containers are fully supported, which substitutes the use of a fully functional operating system. Due to the use of lightweight Linux containers by the Docker, a lot of overhead is reduced. The software comes with its own plugins. For you to get started with this software, you must install it and the VirtualBox. VirtualBox acts as the default provider of Vagrant.

Chapter 2- The Installation process

As mentioned in the previous chapter, before installing vagrant, first install VirtualBox.

Installation of VirtualBox

You need to download the right version of VirtualBox depending on your operating system, and then install it. The PATH variable in this case must be extended by modifying the "*.bash_profile*" file.

```
PATH=$PATH:/Applications/VirtualBox.app/Contents/MacOS/
export PATH
```

The above will act as a guide for Vagrant to know where the installation of the VirtualBox has been done, and this will depend on the operating system that you are using.

Installation of Vagrant

A Vagrant build for a particular operating system can be downloaded and then installed, but if this is not found, it can be installed as gem. This can be done as shown below:

```
S gem install vagrant
```

Creating an instance

You will need to create a directory where Vagrant will be kept. This can be done as follows:

```
mkdir -p ~/Vagrant/project
```

Once created, the above directory can be made into a working directory as follows:

```
cd ~/Vagrant/project
```

Use Ubuntu 12.04 LTS. It usually has the box being set up.

```
vagrant box add precise32 http://files.vagrantup.com/precise32.box
```

Notice the use of the argument *"precise32"*;it will act as a nickname for a particular URL. An instance can then be created thatwill be used to download the box. This can be done as follows:

```
vagrant init precise32
vagrant up
```

At this moment, it is running. In case you want to use SSH to get into the instance, execute the following command:

vagrant ssh

Performing the Configuration

The configuration for the instance will be found in the file *"Vangrantfile"*.This should be as follows:

```
# -*- mode: ruby -*-
# vi: set ft=ruby :

Vagrant::Config.run do|config|
config.vm.box = "precise32"
config.vm.box_url =
"http://files.vagrantup.com/precise32.box"

# Assigning the VM to ahost-only network IP,
allowing for accessing it

# via the IP. Host-only networks may talk to the host
machine and

# any other machines on the same network, but not
accessed
(through this

# network interface) by any external networks.
config.vm.network :hostonly, "192.168.160.10"
# Setting the default project share for using nfs
config.vm.share_folder("v-web", "/vagrant/www",
"./www", :nfs=> true)
```

```
config.vm.share_folder("v-db", "/vagrant/db", "./db",
:nfs=> true)

# Forwarding a port from the guest to host, which will
allow for outside

# computers to access our VM, whereas host only
networking will not.

config.vm.forward_port 80, 8080
# Setting the Timezone to something functional


config.vm.provision    :shell,    :inline=>    "echo
\"Europe/London\"  |  sudo  tee  /etc/timezone  &&
dpkg-reconfigure --frontend noninteractive tzdata"

# Updating the server
config.vm.provision :shell, :inline=> "apt-get update -
-fix-missing"

# Enabling Puppet
config.vm.provision :puppetdo|puppet|


puppet.facter  =  {  "fqdn"=>  "local.pyrocms",
"hostname"=> "www"}

puppet.manifests_path = "puppet/manifests"

puppet.manifest_file    =    "ubuntu-apache2-pgsql-
php5.pp"

puppet.module_path = "puppet/modules"
end
end
```

The above file uses the Ruby syntax, but it shows the basics of the language. The nickname to be used is named, and in case this is not available in the local system, you will use the provided URL.

The lines *"share_folder"* will be used for mapping a folder that is contained in the instance into a local folder. Use of *"nfs=>true"* will have the ability to change permissions and write to files. This feature is of great importance, especially to those who might be trying to install a content management system (CMS) into their system.

With the port forwarding property, the instance will be accessible via**http://localhost:8080**. In case the port brings a conflict, you can change it to another port and this will work too.

Notice that we have also used the configuration file to set the timezone, and we have used the command *"apt-get"*thatwill update the system whenever it is booted. If this stage is not passed, then some packages may fail to install. This is because they will be outdated.

Once the configuration file has been changed, the instance can then be changed to use the following configuration:

vagrant reload

Now, theservers are up and running. You will then install some packages thatyou need. The command *"apt-get install"* can be used for this purpose.

You might be worried by server provisioning. However, this task is oftenleft to sysadmins, so you won't need to worry about it. The idea behind this is to know the kind of software that is installed on your system or the server where development environmentsexist. New staging servers for replication of production and creation of production servers for loadbalancing purpose can also be done.
The issue here is old school provisioning. System administrators have different ways to handle this.

However, there is the issue of modern provisioning. Currently, there are two systems for this purpose, Chef and Puppet. These have been used for a while, and their popularity is increasing. Let's focus on how Puppet works.

With Puppet, youwon't have to write a bunch of commands. Youonly have to build a manifest for Puppet, in which everything to be done is explained. Consider the following command that can be executed on the terminal:

Install Apache

With Puppet, the above command can be written as follows:

Ensure Apache is installed

Alternatively, this could be achieved by creating a folder "*var/www*".Set the permissions to "*www-data:www-data*".You can then use Puppet to say the following:

"Ensure /var/www exists and has permissions matching www-data:www-data"

The difference is that with the manifest, they can be done several times by usingcron jobs, and this will keep things updated. Testing whether everything is running correctly will also be made possible and easy. Errors will be detected and removed rather than waiting for a bunch of commands to do it. In case a component such as PHP does not install, or a configuration fails, an error telling you that will be presented.

Manifests and Modules

A basic manifest is shown below:

```
file {'myfile':
path   => '/tmp/myfile',
ensure => present,
mode   => 0640,
content => "This is my file.",
}
```

In the later manifests, the above file can be referred to as "*myfile*"meaning that you can list it as a dependency for other actions. Consider the following code:

```
include apache
$docroot= '/vagrant/www/pyrocms/'
$db_location= "/vagrant/db/pyrocms.sqlite"
# Setting up Apache
class{'apache::php': }
apache::vhost{ 'local.pyrocms':
priority => '20',
port => '80',
docroot => $docroot,
configure_firewall => false,
}
```

a2mod { 'rewrite': ensure=> present; }

The purpose of the above code is to add the module *"Apache"*, set up some needed variables, running the extra *"apache::php"* manifest in the module Apache, and setting up a virtual host.

PHP also needs to be installed. This is shown below:

```
include php
php::module{ ['xdebug', 'pgsql', 'curl', 'gd'] :
notify => [ Service['httpd'], ],
}
php::conf{ [ 'pdo', 'pdo_pgsql']:
require => Package['php5-pgsql'],
notify  => Service['httpd'],
}
```

With the above code, the PHP extension that you need will be installed on your system. The option *"notify"* will let Apache realize that a new configuration has been made, meaning that a restart of the system will be done. Consider the code shown below:

```
include postgresql
class{'postgresql::server': }
postgresql::db{ 'pyrocms_db':
owner    => 'pyrocms_user',
password => 'password',
}
```

With the above code, the postgres server will be set up, and a database with the name *"pyrocms_db"* will be created. A user with the name *"pyrocms_user"* having the password *"password"* will also be created. You can change the password to any password of your choice.

The last step involves ensuring that the writable files and folders have been set up correctly. This can be done as follows:

```
file { $docroot:
ensure => 'directory',
}
file { "${docroot}system/cms/config/config.php":
ensure => "present",
mode   => "666",
require => File[$docroot],
}

$writeable_dirs= ["${docroot}system/cms/cache/",
"${docroot}system/cms/config/",
"${docroot}addons/", "${docroot}assets/cache/",
"${docroot}uploads/"]
file { $writeable_dirs:
ensure=> "directory",
mode   => '777',
require => File[$docroot],
}
```

The code will ensure that the Apache document root is available, the configuration file will be set to 666, and the writable folders will be set to 777.

You then need to run all of the above. This can be done by restarting Vagrant or running the following command:

```
vagrant provision
```

In this case, the modules PHP, Postgres, and Apache were used. The whole thing can be viewed by cloning the PyroCMSVagrant repo as follows:

```
git clone --recursive git://github.com/pyrocms/devops-vagrant.git ~/vagrant/pyrocms
cd ~/vagrant/pyrocms
vagrant up
```

For you to be able to see the installer, open your browser and then type the following URL:

```
http://localhost:8089/
```

Once you run the above URL, the installer will be seen.

You now know how to set up the VirtualBox, Vagrant, and Puppet server. You also know how to test these to ensure that everything is working correctly and as expected. A checklist for the requirements was created. In the future, you will be able to do this in a short period.

Chapter 3- Boxes in Vagrant

Building virtual machines from scratch is difficult and tedious. With Vagrant, the process is made easy since you use a base image to clone a virtual machine. In Vagrant, the base images are known as *"boxes"*. Once a new Vagrant file is created, you need to specifywhich box it should use.This should be the first step.

Installation of a Box

To add boxes to Vagrant, use the following command:

```
vagrant box add
```

With the above command, the box will be stored under a specific name so that multiple vagrant environments will be in a position to re-use it. In case you haven't added a box, it can be added as follows:

```
$ vagrant box add hashicorp/precise32
```

With the above command, a box with the name "*hashicorp/precise32*" will be downloaded from its site. Note that from this, no box can be found or hosted. A box can also be added from a custom URL, a local file, or others.

Multiple projects can re-use multiple boxes that have been added. A box will be used by each of the projects as the initial image for cloning purposes. Note that the actual base image will not be modified in any way. Suppose that the box "*hashicorp/precise32*"that was added is being used by two projects. Files that are added to one of the guest machines will have no effect on the other guest machine.

Using a Box

Once the box has been added to Vagrant, there is a need to configure the project to use it as the base. Open your Vangrant file and change its contents to the following:

```
Vagrant.configure("2") do |config|

config.vm.box = "hashicorp/precise32"

end
```

The box to be added above should be matched with the "*hashicorp/precise32*".This is how Vagrant discovers the box to be used. It is possible that the box was not added. In this case, Vagrant will download and then install it.

Chapter 4- Up and SSH

Whenever you need to boot the Vagrant environment that you have created run the following command:

```
$ vagrant up
```

Once you execute the above command, you will have your virtual machine up and running the operating system that you used to create it. Notice that in Vagrant, the virtual machine is executed without a user interface, which means that you might not notice that it is running. If you need to prove that it is running, run the following command:

```
$ vagrant ssh
```

With the above command, you will be moved to a session that is using SSH. You can then continue to interact with the virtual machine and do to it whatever that you want. Take care when using the following command:

rm -rf /

Vagrant has a directory named *"/vagrant"* that has the Vagrant file that was created. The above command can delete all of the files contained in the above directory.

Chapter 5- Synced Folders

This feature is used for an automatic synchronizing of folders to and from your guest machine. When it comes to editing files in a virtual machine, many people find it hard to do it over plain editors that are based on the terminal via SSH. In Vagrant, this problem has been solved since the synchronizing will be done automatically.

The default setting of the directory for your project will be shared automatically to the directory *"/vagrant"*, which is located in your guest machine. Note that the directory to be shared has the file *"Vangrantfile"*.

On your machine, execute the commands given below:

```
$ vagrant up
```

The following should is the next command to be executed:

```
$ vagrant ssh
```

This command should give you the following output:

```
vagrant@precise32:~$ ls /vagrant
```

```
Vagrantfile
```

You might wonder about the Vagrant file you find on your virtual machine and the one that you find on the host machine. The two are the same. However, it is good for you to prove this. This can be done by performing a touch on the files, which can be done as follows:

```
vagrant@precise32:~$ touch /vagrant/foo
```

```
vagrant@precise32:~$ exit
```

```
$ ls
```

```
foo Vagrantfile
```

You can now see that the file is in your machine. Notice that the folders have been kept in sync. When you are working with synced folders, you can choose to continue using your text editor on the host machine and this will be synced to the guest machine.

Chapter 6- Networking in Vagrant

You're having your server created, and this server has the ability to modify your files that are located in your host machine and can be synced to the guest machine. Most are not satisfied with accessing web pages from inside the machine by use of the terminal. However, Vagrant offers a feature called *"networking"*, which can be used to access the virtual machine create from your host.

Port Forwarding

This can be used for accessing the virtual machine from the host machine. With this feature, you can specify the ports on the guest machine that can be shared via a port located on the host machine. This means that a port located on the local machine can be accessed. However, all of the traffic will be forwarded to a port located on the guest machine.

Set up a port for forwarding purposes. This should enable youto access Apache, which is located on your guest machine. To do this, edit the Vagrant file located on your system. It should as follows:

```
Vagrant.configure("2") do |config|

config.vm.box = "hashicorp/precise32"

config.vm.provision :shell, path: "bootstrap.sh"

config.vm.network forwarded_port, guest: 80, host:

end
```

You should then apply the changes you have made to the file. This can be done by running the commands:

vagrant up

Or

vagrant reload

You can run any of the above commands. It all depends on whether the machine is running or not. If it is running, use the second command to restart it and if not started, use the first command, which will load it. The changes made will then take effect. Once the machine has been loaded, start your browser and then run the following URL:

http://127.0.0.1:4567

Once you run the above URL, you will notice that a web page whose server is the virtual machine created by Vagrant will be shown.

Private Networks

With private networks, you can access guest machines by use of an IP address, which is not accessible publicly from the global Internet. This means that the IP address assigned to your machine is picked from the available addresses, but within the private address space. Machines thatare contained in the private network can communicate with each other.

DHCP

This is the easiest way a private network can be used, whereby in this case, the IP address of the machine is assigned by the use of DHCP (Domain Host Configuration Protocol). You may not be aware that once youtype a URL in the browser, the URL is assigned an IP address. This is shown below:

Vagrant.configure("2") do |config|
config.vm.network "private_network", type: "dhcp"
end

With the above code, the IP addresses will be picked from the reserved space of IP addresses. If you need to determine the IP address, run the following command to SSH:

---

vagrant ssh

Note that the above command should be executed in the actual machine and theappropriate tool such as the *"ifconfig"* can be used to learn the IP.

Static IP

A static IP address for your machine can be specified. This is an indication that the machine managed by Vagrant will be accessible via the static IP. The Vagrant file that belongs to a static IP address should be as follows:

Vagrant.configure("2") do |config|
config.vm.network "private_network", ip:
"192.168.160.4"
end

The users are then left with the task of making sure that the IP address they use on their machine does not collide with that of the other machines on the network.

Although it is possible for you to use the IP of your choice, it must be selected from the ones available in the private IP address space. When you do this, there is a guarantee that the IP will never be routed publicly, and the routers will have the capability to block traffic coming from the outside world. If you use a static IP address in some operating systems, you will be prompted to provide other settings such as the default gateway and others, so make sure that you specify the values for these.

Disabling Auto-Configuration

You might need to configure the network on your own, rather than letting Vagrant do it automatically. In this case, the feature *"auto_config"* needs to be changed. This can be done as follows:

```
Vagrant.configure("2") do |config|

config.vm.network "private_network", ip: "192.168.160.4",

auto_config: false

end

vagrant up
```

In case the Vagrant environment is started without having set the *"auto-config"*, the files that are placed will still be there. To remove, do it manually by deleting them. You can choose to destroy and then recreate the virtual machine.

Public Networks

These networks provide less privacy compared to private networks. With public networks, members of the public are allowed to access your machine.

DHCP

If you allow the DHCP to assign an IP address on your behalf, your work will be easier. A public network can then be defined as follows:

```
Vagrant.configure("2") do |config|

config.vm.network "public_network"

end
```

If the DHCP has been used and you need to determine the IP, use the following command to SSH:

vagrant ssh

The command should be executed on the appropriate machine on the command line tool and an appropriate command, such as *"ifconfig"*, can be used to show the IP.

Static IP

Sometimes, people wish to manually set the IP address for their bridge interface. To do this, the clause *"ip"* can be added to the IP configuration as shown below:

```
config.vm.network "public_network", ip: "192.168.160.17"
```

Default Network Interface

It is possible that your machine will have multiple network interfaces. In this case, you will be asked by Vagrant to specify which interface to use while bridging the virtual machine. To specify a default interface, use the clause *":bridge"* in the definition of the network. This is shown below:

```
config.vm.network "public_network", bridge: "en1: Wi-Fi (AirPort)"
```

The string used for the name of the interface should match the exact interface that is currently available. In case the interface you specify is not found, the available interfaces will be presented to, you and you will be asked to pick the correct one. Some providers will allow you to specify the list of adapters you can bridge against. This is shown below:

```
config.vm.network "public_network", bridge: [

"en1: Wi-Fi (AirPort)",

"en6: Broadcom NetXtreme Gigabit Ethernet Controller",

]

config.vm.network "public_network"

end
```

In the above case, the first network adapter to be found will be used if it can be bridged successfully.

Disabling Auto-Configuration

You might need to perform the configuration on your own, that is, the configuration of the interface. In this case, you have to disable the auto-configuration property. This can be done as shown below:

```
Vagrant.configure("2") do |config|

config.vm.network "public_network", auto_config: false

end
```

After that, you can use the shell provisioner for configuration of the IP for the interface. This can be done as shown below:

```
Vagrant.configure("2") do |config|
config.vm.network "public_network", auto_config:
false
# manual IP configuration
config.vm.provision "shell",
run: "always",
inline: "ifconfig eth1 192.168.160.17 netmask
255.255.255.0 up"
# manual ipv6
config.vm.provision "shell",
run: "always",
inline: "ifconfig eth1 inet6 add fc00::17/7"
end
```

Default Router

There might be a need for you to override the default
configuration of your router, which will depend on your setup.
This is needed if you are required to access the Vagrant box
from other networks or a public network. This can be done by
use of the shell provisioner script as it is shown below:

```
config.vm.network "public_network", ip:
"192.168.160.17"
# default router
config.vm.provision "shell",
```

```
run: "always",
inline: "route add default gw 192.168.160.1"
# default router ipv6
config.vm.provision "shell",
run: "always",
inline: "route -A inet6 add default gw fc00::1 eth1"
# delete default gw on eth0
config.vm.provision "shell",
run: "always",
inline: "eval `route -n | awk '{ if ($8 ==\"eth0\" && $2
!= \"0.0.0.0\") print \"route del default gw \" $2; }'`"
```

The above code is specific to a particular operating system, but it is good that you have an idea of how it can be done.

Chapter 7- Multi-Machine

With Vagrant, youcan control and define several virtual machines per each of the available Vagrant files. This is an idea referred to as a *"multi-machine"* environment. The machines will be in a position to work together and they will be closely associated to each other.

Definition of multiple machines

The definition of multiple machines can be done in the Vagrant file of the project by use of a method call named *"config.vm.define"*. With this method call, a Vagrant file definition is done within another Vagrant file definition. Consider the example given below:

```
Vagrant.configure("2") do |config|
config.vm.provision "shell", inline: "echo Hello there"
config.vm.define "web" do |web|
web.vm.box = "apache"
end
config.vm.define "database" do |database|
database.vm.box = "mysql"
end
end
```

The "*config.vm.define*" will take a block with another variable. With Vagrant, ordering-in is enforced. This is demonstrated in the example given below:

```
Vagrant.configure("2") do |config|
config.vm.provision :shell, inline: 'echo Apple'
config.vm.define :testing do |test|
test.vm.provision :shell, inline: 'echo Boy'
end
config.vm.provision :shell, inline: 'echo Cow'
end
```

The above program should output the following when executed:

Apple

Cow

Boy

Note that "*Boy*"is the last output. This is because an outside-in ordering in the file above was used.

Specification of a primary machine

It is possible to specify a particular machine as the primary one. After specifying this in a multi-machine environment, when you fail to specify a default machine to be used, the primary machine will be used as the default.

To define primary machines use the keyword *"primary"* during its definition. This is shown below:

config.vm.define "web", primary: true do |web|
 # ...
End

Auto-start Machines

Running the command *"vagrant up"* in a multi-machine environment will lead to launching all of the defined machines. Use *"autostart"* to tell Vagrant not to start certain machines when the above command is executed. An example of this is given below:

```
config.vm.define "web"

config.vm.define "database"

config.vm.define "database_follower", autostart: false
```

When the command *"vagrant up"* is executed with the above setting, only the machines *"web"* and *"database"* will be started. Therefore, the machine *"database_follower"* will not be started. The reason for this is that the auto start value for this is set to *"false"*. However, it is possible for you to force this machine to restart. This can be done by executing the following command:

```
vagrant up database_follower
```

This will start the machine that isn't started.

Chapter 8- Providers

Vagrant supports other types of machines. This can be achieved by using Vagrant together with providers. Some providers will offer you features that are meaningful and important to you. A good example of this is Vmware, which is more stable and highly supported compared to the VirtualBox.

For you to be able to use any other provider, you must first install it. For you to install any other provide other than the VirtualBox, you must use the Vagrant plugin system. It is after this installation that you can begin to use the provider.

Installation

To install plugins use the command *"vagrant plugin install"*. This is shown below:

```
$ vagrant plugin install vagrant-example-plugin
```

The installation process will take seconds. Once the installation is completed, Vagrant will load it automatically. If some plugins fail to install, they should not crash Vagrant. Instead, an error message saying that plugin failed to load will notify you. For you to update plugins, you should use the following command:

```
$ vagrant plugin update
```

With the above command, all of the plugins installed on your system will be updated to the latest version. You might also need to update a specific plugin. Its name can be used as follows for this purpose:

```
$ vagrant plugin update NAME
```

Plugins that are updated will be shown together with their latest version.

Uninstallation

A plugin can easily be uninstalled. The following command can be used:

```
$ vagrant plugin uninstall
```

The command removes the plugin from your system. Consider the example given below:

```
$ vagrant plugin uninstall vagrant-example-plugin
```

If you need to see the list of plugins that are installed in your Vagrant system, do use the following command:

$ vagrant plugin list

With the above command, all of the plugins and their version will be shown.

Commands for Plugin Development

To define new commands within the context of plugin definition, do the following:

command "command_name" do
require_relative "command"
Command
End

To define commands in Vagrant use the *"command"* method as shown above. The method takes the passed argument as the name of the command. In this case, it is *"command_name"*. To invoke the command execute the following:

"vagrant command_name".

Non-primary commands can also be defined. They will not show up in the output *"vagrant –h"*. If you need to be able to see them, execute the following command:

```
$ vagrant list-commands
```

This is useful for commands new to Vagrant. For Vagrant to expose some of its internal functions, it uses non-primary commands.

If you need to define a non-primary command, use the following method:

```
command("foo", primary: false) do

require_relative "command"

Command

end
```

Implementation

Consider the following example that show how commands can be implemented in Vagrant:

```
class Command < Vagrant.plugin(2, :command)
def execute
puts "Hello there!"
0
end
end
```

Notice the use of the subclass *"Vagrant.plugin(2, :command)"*.Once the command has been executed, the method *"execute"* will be called. This should provide you with the exit status of the code. Zero is for success while any other output will be an error.

Parsing options to the command-line

You can use the method *"parse_options"* to parse the command line. The *"OptionParser"* is used as the argument, and common elements will be added to it. An example of common elements is the flag *"—help"*. This is used for giving help once it has been requested. Consider the example given below:

```
options = {}
options[:force] = false
op = OptionParser.new do |o|
o.banner = "Usage: vagrant destroy [vm-name]"
o.separator ""
o.on("-f", "--force", "Destroying without a
confirmation.") do |f|
options[:force] = f
end
end
# Parsing the options
argv = parse_options(op)
```

Use of Vagrant Machines

The method "*with_target_vms*" helps interact with virtual machines managed by Vagrant in a standard Vagrant way. If you are in a multi-machine environment, then this method will do the right thing on your behalf and target machines will be handled in the command line. For you to perform a manipulation of a Vagrant machine, you should use the helper. The following example illustrates how a helper can be used:

```
with_target_vms(argv, reverse: true) do |machine|

machine.action(:destroy)

end
```

In this case, the machines will be asked for in reverse order. A destroy action will then be called on each of them. Consider the following case:

```
vagrant destroy command_name
```

When the user says the above command, the helper function will launch the *"command_name"* machine. In case you do not provide parameters to the method and the environment is a multi-machine one, every machine contained in the environment will be yielded and the process will be continued. The right thing for the environment will be done.

You might also need to use the Raw Vagrant environment. In this case, you should use the object *"Vagrant::Environment"* that can be made available by use of the instance variable*"@env"*.

Configuration

Some users of VirtualBox choose to turn to VMware. With VMware, you can configure some additional settings to accomplish some complex tasks.

Locating "VMware FUSION.APP"

By default, the VMware Fusion will be looked for in "/Applications" and in "~/Applications".

If the applications are put in any other directory, you will be forced to use a manual method to tell VMware where to find the Fusion. To do this, use the environment variable "VAGRANT_VMWARE_FUSION_APP".

An example of this is when your applications have been put in the directory "/App".Vagrant should be configured as follows:

```
$ export VAGRANT_VMWARE_FUSION_APP="/Apps/VMware Fusion.app"
$ vagrant up --provider=vmware_fusion
```

Virtual Machine GUI

With the VMware provider, the virtual machines will be started in headless mode. In case you need to see the user interface since you are running your desktop ina virtual machine, or you need to debug issues that have potential to affect the virtual machine, the VMware provider can be configured to boot with the GUI. This is shown below:

```
config.vm.provider "vmware_fusion" do |v|

v.gui = true

end
```

If a VMware work stations are being used, and then use *"vmware_workstation"*.

Customizing VMX

You might need to remove or add some keys from the VMX file. This can be done as follows:

config.vm.provider "vmware_fusion" do |v|
v.vmx["custom-key"] = "value"
v.vmx["another-key"] = nil
end

If the workstation being used is a VMware one, use the *"vmware_workstation"*. With the example shown above set the property *"custom_key"* to *"value"*. The key *"another-key"* will be removed from our VMX file.

Customization of VMX will be the last step to be performed once the VMware machine has been booted. This means that you are able to change the configuration or undo the ones made to Vagrant.

The format for VMX is undocumented, and for the available values and keys, there is no official way to reference them.

For the case of the keys, most people look for the ones for setting both the CPU and memory. The example given below shows how these two can be set:

```
config.vm.provider "vmware_fusion" do |v|

v.vmx["memsize"] = "1024"

v.vmx["numvcpus"] = "3"

end
```

Kernel Upgrade

Whenever Vagrant and the VMware are running together, there is a need for you to perform an upgrade of the kernel. When this done, the guest tools for VMware will stop working. The features of Vagrant, such as networking and synced folders, will be rendered nonfunctional.

In this section, we will show you how the kernel can be upgraded while leaving the networking tools working effectively.

Enabling Auto-Upgrade of VMware tools

If the operating system you are running is a common one, the tools for VMware can upgrade on their own. However, the system comes with this setting disabled by default. Consider the following settings of the Vagrant file. This will enable the auto-upgrade of this:

```
# Ensureing that the VMWare Tools recompiles
kernel modules
# whenever the linux images are updated
$fix_vmware_tools_script = <<SCRIPT


sed -i.bak 's/answer
AUTO_KMODS_ENABLED_ANSWER no/answer
AUTO_KMODS_ENABLED_ANSWER yes/g'
/etc/vmware-tools/locations

sed -i 's/answer AUTO_KMODS_ENABLED
no/answer AUTO_KMODS_ENABLED yes/g'
/etc/vmware-tools/locations
SCRIPT


Vagrant.configure(2) do |config|
# ...
config.vm.provision "shell", inline:
$fix_vmware_tools_script
end
```

You need to know that the above will not work in every operating system being used by users. Once the above changes are made, you need to make them take effect. This can only be done by reloading the system, in which case, you should use either of the following commands depending on the status of your system:

```
vagrant up

vagrant reload
```

Once the above is done, test your synch folders, and if they are found to be working, then you will be set.

Chapter 9- Plugins

Vagrant comes with many features users will find interesting. However, you might not be interested in some of its features, or you might need to change how it works. You might also be interested in adding some particular functionality to it. These can only be implemented by use of the plugins, which will be explored in this chapter.

Developing plugins

These enable us to improve or add functionality to Vagrant. However, they must be used with external dependencies from the users. This means that they should only be used as a last resort.

They are packaged into RubyGem, meaning they need to developed like RubyGem. Use the following command for this purpose:

```
bundle gem
```

Once the directory setup for the RubyGem has been set up, the Gemfile should then be modified. The Gemfile for developing a Vagrant plugin should be as follows:

```
source "https://rubygems.org"
group :development do
gem "vagrant", git:
"https://github.com/mitchellh/vagrant.git"
end
group :plugins do
gem "my-vagrant-plugin", path: "."
end
```

For the sake of development, the Gemfile will get Vagrant. You can then run Vagrant with the plugin already reloaded by use of the following command:

```
bundle exec vagrant
```

This will enable you to test the file manually.

Plugin Definition

It is necessary that all of the plugins be defined. In the definition, the details of the plugin, such as its name and the components it contains, should be described. The following is an example of the definition can be done:

class MyPlugin < Vagrant.plugin("2")
name "My Plugin"
end

The definition itself inherits from the class *"Vagrant.plugin("2")"*. The two in the syntax shows the version of the plugin. Each version of the plugin will be compatible with the API.

Components of Plugins

During the definition of a Vagrant plugin, the components added to Vagrant are defined. Consider the example given below, in which a command and a provisioner are added:

```
class MyPlugin < Vagrant.plugin("2")
name "New Plugin"

command "run-my-plugin" do
require_relative "command"
Command
end
provisioner "my-provisioner" do
require_relative "provisioner"
Provisioner
end
end
```

The syntax and semantics used in the above code belong to the Ruby programming language.

Commands for Plugin Development

To define new commands within the context of plugin definition, use the syntax given below:

```
command "name" do

require_relative "command"

Command

end
```

To define commands use the method *"command"*. The argument for this method is the name of the command. The command will then be invoked as follows:

```
vagrant name
```

For the case of plugins, non-primary commands, which do not show up in *"vagrant –h"* output can be defined as shown below:

```
command("name", primary: false) do
require_relative "command"
Command
End
```

For the case of the implementation of the commands, the procedure is very simple. You only have to implement a single method, which is the method *"execute"*. This is shown in the example given below:

```
class Command < Vagrant.plugin(2, :command)
def execute
puts "Hello there!"
o
end
end
```

Once the command is invoked, call the *"execute"* method. This should then give the exit status of the code, and zero means a success. Any other output is an indication of an error

Chapter 10- Command-line Interface

To interact with Vagrant, this should be done via the command line. You then need to know most of its commands.

Connect

This command enables access to shared environments. It takes the following syntax:

vagrant connect NAME

Consider the following options given for the command:

disable-static-ip

Once the above option has been set, you will be forced to use the SOCKS proxy address to access the connection. Note that with the connect command; a small virtual machine will not be able to spin to create an IP address to be accessed. This flag solves this problem.

Consider the option given below:

--static-ip IP

The option (-ip) tells to connect command the static IP address to be used for the virtual machine. If not specified, the default one, which is in the space 172.16.0.0/16 will be used. Consider the next option given below:

ssh

If the above option is used in an environment shared with the "vagrant share –ssh", then connection to the environment will be established by use of SSH.

Destroy

The command takes the following syntax:

```
vagrant destroy
```

With this command, the Vagrant machines that are running will be stopped. All of the resources created during the Vagrant machine creation process will also be destroyed. Once the command runs, the computer will be left clean. It will look as if no guest machine was created. However, before the destruction of the virtual machines, you will be asked for a confirmation.

If you need to skip this confirmation, use the flag "$-f$" or "*force*". However, if there is a box created during the command "*vagrant up*", then this box will not be destroyed. This means that the box will be left in the hard drive. If you need to restore the computer to the state it was at before executing the command, you have to run the following command:

vagrant box remove

Global Status

This command takes the following syntax:

vagrant global-status

With this command, you are able to learn the status of the Vagrant environments currently active for the user who is currently logged in. The function of this command is based on the cache rather than performing an actual evaluation of the listed machine. This means that stale results can be observed.

For the purpose of pruning entries that are not important. This can be done by use of the following flag:

--prune

In the output, you will observe an ID that is "*a1b2c3*".With this ID, you can control the Vagrant machine from anywhere in the system. Any of the Vagrant commands used to take a target machine can work together with the ID. An example of this is given below:

vagrant destroy a1b2c3

In any case, your environment fails to show up, execute the following commands in the stated order:

vagrant destroy

vagrant up

In case you performed an upgrade from the earlier version of Vagrant, the environments in existence will not show up in the global status until you destroy and then recreate them. This command has only one option, which is "*prune*" and has been shown on the previous page.

Login

The command takes the following syntax:

```
vagrant login
```

The command is used for user authentication by use of the HarshiCorp's Atlas server. The process of logging only becomes necessary when accessing protected boxes using Vagrant Share.

For you to use Vagrant, logging in is not a requirement. Note that this feature is necessary only in some features such as the protected boxes. The command takes the following options.

--check

The above flag is used to check whether you are logged into the system. If you are logged in, it will return a zero while if you are not logged in, it will return a one.

--logout

With the above flag, the user will be logged out of the system if they are logged in. However, if you are already logged out of the system, the command will do nothing, but it will not produce an error.

--token

With this flag, the Atlas login token will be manually set to the string that you provide. The assumption is that the token is a relevant Atlas access token. Consider the examples given:

If you need to use the username and password to securely authenticate to Atlas, this can be done as follows:

```
$ vagrant login
# ...
Atlas username:
Atlas password:
```

If you need to check whether the user who is currently logged in is authenticated or not, execute the following command:

```
$ vagrant login --check
You are already logged in.
```

To authenticate yourself securely with Atlas by use of a token, this can be done as follows:

```
S vagrant login --token WXYZ1234

The token was successfully saved.
```

RDP

This command takes the following syntax:

vagrant rdp

With this command, a RDP client will be started, and this will be for a remote desktop having the guest machine. However, you need to know that this can only be supported in environments where remote desktops are supported. This means only the Windows Operating system.

Raw Arguments

You can use the command line to pass raw arguments to your RDP client. This can be appended to the symbol "- -". Vagrant will pass these. An example is given below:

```
$ vagrant rdp -- /span
```

When the above command is run on Windows, "mstsc.exe /span config.rdp" will be executed. This means that your RDP will then be in a position to span multiple desktops.

Chapter 11- Vagrant Push

Version 1.7 of Vagrant brought many improvements to the Vagrant community. It is now possible for you to deploy or push application code into the same directory as the Vagrant file to a server located remotely, and this will be invoked by use of the following command:

vagrant push

Definition of the pushes is done in the Vagrant file, and to invoke these, use the command *"vagrant push"*. Each of the plugins for Vagrant Push has its own configuration options. Consider the following section of the Vagrant file that shows how Vagrant Push can be configured:

```
config.push.define "ftp" do |push|

push.host = "ftp.company.com"

push.username = "..."

# ...

end
```

Once the application is ready for deployment into the ftp server, the following single command should be executed:

```
$ vagrant push
```

With Vagrant push, multiple backend declarations are supported. An example of this is given below:

```
config.push.define "staging", strategy: "ftp" do |push|

#  ...

end

config.push.define "qa", strategy: "ftp" do |push|

#  ...

end
```

In this case, the name of the Vagrant Push must be passed to the subcommand as shown below:

```
$ vagrant push staging
```

Vagrant Push makes the process of deploying applications much easier to use when doing this.

Conclusion

It can be concluded that Vagrant is computer software used for creation and configuration of virtual environments. Before version 1.1 of this software was released, it was highly tied to VirtualBox, which is virtualization software. However, with the release of this version of the software, users are now able to work with other virtualization software, such as the VMware and the KVM. This shows how flexible and useful Vagrant has become.

The software is now supported in server environments, which is an indication that it can be used in production environments. Also, note that Vagrant was developed by use of the Ruby programming languages. Many people think that because of this, the software cannot support projects written in other programming languages. However, this is not the case since this software can support projects written in programming languages such as Python, Java, and C#. It also has full support for Docker containers. This has greatly reduced the overhead involved in the use of Linux containers.

The process of installing the Docker is very simple. However, you need to begin by installing VirtualBox. You then have to download the right version of the Vagrant software depending on the operating system you are using. The installation process of Vagrant should then be followed. To create an instance of the software, create a new directory and then use it for this purpose. Whenever you make changes to your Vagrant software, you have to restart the system so that the changes can take effect. With boxes, the process of building virtual machines has been made much easier. This is because the process is done by use of base images, which are the boxes.

Thank you!

We would like to thank you for buying this book. Hope you found it helpful in your now EASY and FAST programming life development. And we are happy to recommend you some other books from this author:

ANDROID PROGRAMMING: Complete Introduction for Beginners -Step By Step Guide How to Create Your Own Android App Easy!

ANDROID GAME PROGRAMMING: COMPLETE INTRODUCTION FOR BEGINNERS: STEP BY STEP GUIDE HOW TO CREATE YOUR OWN ANDROID APP EASY!

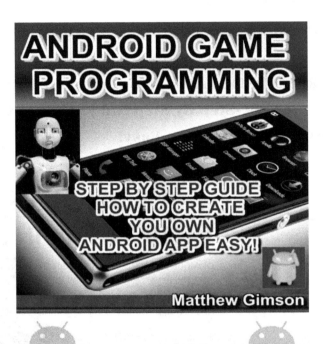

Linux Command Line: FAST and EASY! (Linux Commands, Bash Scripting Tricks, Linux Shell Programming Tips and Bash One-Liners)

Linux Command Line: Become a Linux Expert! (Input/Output Redirection, Wildcards, File Security, Processes Managing, Shell Programming Advanced Features, GUI elements, Useful Linux Commands)

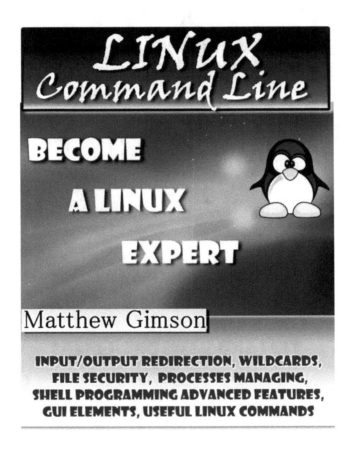

PHP and MySQL Programming for Beginners: A Step by Step Course From Zero to Professional

DOCKER: Everything You Need to Know to Master Docker (Docker Containers, Linking Containers, Whalesay Image, Docker Installing on Mac OS X and Windows OS)

Docker: Docker Guide for Production Environment (Programming is Easy Book 8)

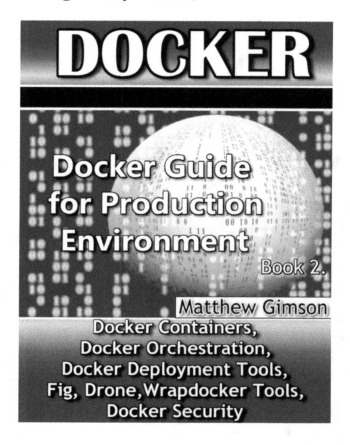

Excel VBA Programming: Learn Excel VBA Programming FAST and EASY! (Programming is Easy Book 9)

VAGRANT: Make Your Life Easier With VAGRANT. Master VAGRANT FAST and EASY! (Programming is Easy Book 10)

SCALA PROGRAMMING: Learn Scala Programming FAST and EASY! (Programming is Easy Book 11)

NODE. JS: Practical Guide for Beginners (Programming is Easy Book 12)

IOS 8 APP DEVELOPMENT. Develop Your Own App FAST and EASY!